Little Raccoon

Little Raccoon
SUZANNE NOGUERE
illustrated by TONY CHEN

Holt, Rinehart and Winston
New York

Library of Congress Cataloging in Publication Data
Noguere, Suzanne.
  Little Raccoon.

  SUMMARY: Throughout the first year of her life,
Little Raccoon gradually matures until she is ready
to be on her own.
  1. Raccoons—Juvenile literature. 2. Animals,
Infancy of—Juvenile literature. [1. Raccoons]
I. Chen, Tony. II. Title.
QL737.C26N63   599.74'443   80-26171
ISBN 0-03-054826-8

For my mother   SN

For Pura   TC

It was early May, when raccoons have babies. This one walked through the forest looking for a den for her babies to be born in. An empty tree hole would be the best. But it had to be big because she might have as many as seven cubs, and it had to be near fresh water. A cave, a crevice in a rock, or a woodchuck burrow would also make a good den. High in a maple tree the raccoon found a good hollow.

The next day, she was the mother of four cubs, one female and three males. They would not open their eyes for three weeks. Mother fed them her milk. For two months, that was all the food they would need. At night, when raccoons are active, Mother left the den to find food for herself. Little Raccoon and her three brothers were alone. But they were safe from their enemies—the bobcat, the red fox, the great horned owl, and hunters with dogs.

At dawn, when Mother came back, the cubs twittered like birds. They were hungry. Mother sat on her haunches and held them up to her breasts. They sucked her milk eagerly and purred. Then the family slept the day away. Three weeks later, the cubs opened their eyes. Little Raccoon saw her brothers for the first time. They had gray fur, black masks that hid their black eyes, and plump tails with black rings. Her own fur was brown.

For the whole month of June, Little Raccoon and all baby raccoons in North America did nothing but nurse, sleep, and grow. But raccoons are curious and playful; and soon Little Raccoon and her brothers were getting into trouble.

One dawn, Mother returned carrying a crab claw. The cubs thought it was a toy and tugged at it with all their might. Little Raccoon's hands slipped. She fell out of the tree and landed on the forest floor with a plop! Her brothers stared down at her but couldn't

help. They hadn't yet learned how to climb. Little Raccoon started to cry. Mother climbed down the tree, picked her up in her mouth, and carried her home. Little Raccoon had had a fright. She was glad to snuggle up and be good, if only for a while.

After that, the cubs learned how to climb. One July night, when they were two months old, Mother made a trilling sound in her throat, telling the cubs to follow her. She led them to a pond to teach them how to find food. On the way, Little Raccoon stopped to examine the sights. Mother missed her and ran back. She found Little Raccoon sitting in a berry patch, squishing berries and licking

the juice off her fingers. Mother gave her a good scolding and led her back to the pond.

Mother stood in the shallow water. Staring off into the distance, she dipped her hands in the water and, like magic, pulled out a crayfish. She had caught it without looking! The cubs followed her example, feeling under the stones for crayfish.

Their keen sense of touch told them
what every object was. Soon they were
making magic of their own.
Little Raccoon ate a crayfish,
her first solid food.

That is how the raccoon got its name. The Powhatan Indians of Virginia called it *ara-kun*, which means "he who scratches with his hands." Little Raccoon caught another crayfish and dipped it in and out of the water. She was not washing her food, just enjoying how it felt in her hands.

Each summer night, Mother showed the cubs a different part of their home range. They explored all the land within a mile or two of the tree where they had been born. The family no longer slept there. When dawn came, they slept wherever they liked, in another tree or on the ground.

One night, Mother led the cubs to a swamp. On the way, Little Raccoon spotted a moving cricket and stopped to watch it. She did not notice two cold lights, too close to be stars, gleaming above her. They were the eyes of a bobcat. The bobcat watched and waited, quiet as the moon, then sprang!

Little Raccoon squealed in terror. Mother heard the cry and came running. She was not very big, weighing just fifteen pounds; but, like all grown raccoons, she was very, very

strong. No one in the forest wanted to fight
with her. She slashed out at the bobcat with
her claws. Instantly, he dropped Little Raccoon and went away.

The next night, Little Raccoon stayed close to her family when they went looking for food. She and her brothers ate everything, animals and plants. Mother taught the cubs how to find frogs, mice, earthworms, and other good things to eat.

Late one September day, Little Raccoon and a brother saw something new. It was a honeybee. They chased it to a hollow tree and climbed up.

Something smelled good in there. Little Raccoon reached in and pulled out some honeycomb. A bee guarding the nest stung her hand! It hurt, but not enough to drive her away from the delicious honey. Hundreds of bees flew out and buzzed wildly around the two masked bandits. That didn't stop them. They ate their fill and went on their way.

A favorite food was corn. At summer's end, the raccoon family raided a cornfield. The farmer's dogs caught their scent and began to bark. Little Raccoon wasn't able to run; she had eaten too much. So Mother pushed all the cubs up a tree for safety and ran to a stream. The dogs followed her scent. She had tricked them into it. Mother plunged into the stream and swam away. Her scent disappeared at the water's edge. When she went

back to her cubs, she found them safe and
sound in the tree. As the family left, they
could still hear the dogs barking in the distance, trying to find Mother's scent.

At four months, Little Raccoon no longer
needed her mother's milk. She found all her
own food. She knew enough to go off alone at
night. Sometimes she slept alone.

In October, the leaves
turned red and yellow.
Acorns, chestnuts,
beechnuts, and apples
fell from the trees.

Little Raccoon ate nuts and apples to her heart's content. She ate so much that she got fat. She had to. That was her fuel for the winter ahead.

As the weather grew colder, the cubs went back to sleeping with Mother. In late November, when it turned very cold, the whole family moved into a tree den for the winter.

Little Raccoon slept away the coldest weeks, warm in her thick coat, with her bushy tail for a cover. While she slept, her body burned up her fat for fuel.

During a warm spell, she woke up, went outside looking for food, then returned to the den to sleep some more.

At the end of February, Mother left the den to mate. Then she went back to her cubs. In nine weeks, she would give birth to new cubs.

By March, Little Raccoon was almost starved. She had used up all her fat. As soon as it grew warm, she and her family left the den. They felt about in the melting snow for food and ate soggy acorns.